FINANCIAL WELL-BEING

SOLUTIONS TO DRIVE IMPROVED FINANCIAL WELLBEING AND BEHAVIOURAL CHANGE

ALEXIA BRANDY

copyright ©2021 Alexia Brandy

All Right Reserved

TABLE OF CONTENTS

INTRODUCTION

CHAPTER ONE
INVESTMENT GOALS
MID-TERM GOALS
SHORT-TERM GOAL
LONG-TERM GOALS
LIFE STAGES
RISK AND RETURN

CHAPTER TWO
EASY AREAS YOU NEED TO FIGURE ON BEFORE ESCAPING THE CORPORATE WORLD (LEARN FROM THE BEST)

CHAPTER THREE
THE ULTIMATE TRUTH MOST PEOPLE IGNORE THAT WILL DETERMINE YOUR LEVEL OF SUCCESS

CHAPTER FOUR
THE ONE OBSESSION ALL SUCCESSFUL PEOPLE SHARE THAT COMPLETELY DESTORYS PROCRASTINATION

CHAPTER FIVE
THE SCIENCE OF GETTING RICH

CHAPTER SIX
TO LIVE COMPLETELY IN THE SOUL, MAN SHOULD HAVE LOVE; AND LOVE IS DENIED ARTICULATION BY DESTITUTION

Chapter Seven

PERPETUALLY FOLLOWS THE DOING OF THINGS IN THE SPECIFIC MANNER

INTRODUCTION

The major difference between those that succeed and people who fail is simple. Every Successful people in every field are goal getter and action-oriented, while failures are talk-oriented. People that achieve greatly are those that just do it! While those that accomplish little spend their lives hoping, wishing, dreaming and making excuses. By Reading this book, you've step into the ranks of those few who make things happen, instead of those who await things to happen to them.

What you're about to learn will have positive impact your life. These insights, ideas and methods are the drive to financial success for millions of young and old, rich and poor. These principles are simple, effective, and fairly easy to use. This method has been tested and its works and they will work for you if you'll take them and apply them in your own life.

This generation is the best in human history. Many people are becoming wealthy today, starting from nothing, than ever before imagined.

There are more than 20 millionaires in America, most of them are self-made, and therefore the number is growing by 25 to 28 percent annually. We even have self-made millionaires and billionaires.

This type of rapid wealth creation has never been seen in human history.

Here's the best news of all. Virtually everyone starts with nothing. Quite 90 percent of all successful people today started off broke or nearly broke. The average self-made millionaire has been bankrupt or nearly bankrupt 5 times. Most wealthy people failed repeatedly before they finally found the right opportunity that they were able to leverage into financial success. And what many thousands and millions of other people have done, you'll do it.

There is a powerful Quote. It says that there's a selected effect for each cause for each action, there is a reaction. This law says that success isn't an accident. Financial success is the cause of doing certain, specific things over and over again until you achieve the financial independence that you simply desire. Nature is neutral. The natural world, the market-place, or our society does not care who you are or what you're.

If you are doing what other successful people do, you'll eventually get the results that other successful people get. And if you don't, you won't. Once you learn the secrets of millionaires and apply them in your own life, you'll experience results and rewards far beyond anything you've got accomplished up so far.

Here are the key points for you to remember. Nobody smarter or better than you. You need to develop trust in yourself. The key to putting together trust is to be trustworthy and therefore the key to trusting yourself is to be faithful to yourself.

The Difference Between Rich and Poor the rich aren't very different from you and me. They have simply used more of their god-given talents and done things during a different way from the majority. The wonderful discovery is this: if you are doing what other successful, wealthy people do, repeatedly, you'll eventually get an equivalent and amazing results. It's not a miracle, neither is it luck. If you initiate the causes, you'll get the result.

This book explained deeply on the concept of well-being from many ways, bringing together the voices of long-time champions of monetary capability and newer voices hailing from a spread of sectors, like public health and business. What unites them is that the shared recognition that we must do more to assist all Americans has control over their financial lives and achieves their financial goals. As been stated clearly on the cover of this book, financial well-being is that the bridge to a robust financial future, connecting individuals and families to greater opportunity, creating more serene environment, and successively, strengthening the social and economic fabric of our nation. In the states , they defined financial status by income or wealth, but experts in policy and practice from a variety of fields are expanding our focus to raised understand what consumers actually want and wish in their financial lives. A consensus is emerging that satisfaction with one's financial life has elements that are both objective (income, wealth, cash flow) and subjective (financial freedom, on target to satisfy financial goals). Financial health is deeply tied to the supply of opportunity, which too often depends on factors outside an individual's control, like race, parental socioeconomic status, and macroeconomic climate.

You should be able to determine the way you want your wealth to work. Whatever your purpose is in life, careful planning and successful investing of your wealth can assist you get there in no time. We'll walk you through the opportunities and challenges you are facing. The starting line is to define exactly what you would like to get out of your investments, set realistic targets and focus on them.

Goals-based investing places your goals right at the middle of the recommendation process.

CHAPTER ONE

Investment goals

Setting your specific investment goals also will keep you focused once you need it and enable you to create a portfolio of savings and investments to urge you where you would like to be. Investment strategies should include a mixture of varied investment and fund types so as to get a balanced approach to risk and return.

Maintaining a balanced approach is typically key to the probabilities of achieving your investment goals, while bearing in mind that at some point you'll want access to your money. This makes it important to permit for "edibility in your planning.

There is a spread of reasons why you would possibly prefer to invest. Some investment goals could also be open-ended, while others may accompany a selected deadline. Also as understanding what your goals are, you furthermore may got to believe once you hope to realize them. These will typically range from build up a deposit for a property, or planning for your children's future education expenses, to retirement planning. Managing these competing interests requires you to seem at each of your financial objectives both individually and as an entire.

Life stages

With much anticipation, the targeted goal which is considered short, medium, and long term is shifting, more so for every individual. This is often because someone in their mid-25s today might spend 50 to 55 years working then has 35 years in retirement. So those in their 25s and 30s might want to think about medium-term objectives to be between ten and 30 years and long term as anything over 35 years. Recognizing when it's appropriate to take a position and when it's better to save lots of money in cash to satisfy your different goals is extremely important. generally, anything you'll need money for in five years or less is seen as short-term, while goals set five to 10 years from now are considered mid-term while Long-term goals are usually those that you'll need money in 20 or more years.

Short-term goals

Achieving Short-term goals in the period of 2 to 5 years, like buying a brand new car or vacation, is the reason for cash savings. This is because investing in a stock exchange over short time frames exposes you to a potential risk, and if the market falls you'll have little time to recoup any reductions in your money. If you're only saving or investing for a comparatively short period of your time, you would like more certainty about how your savings and investments will perform, and for your money to be easily accessible.

Mid-term goals

The medium-term investment is an investment span of 5 to 10 years. Your goal is more than a short-term investment, though it's not within the distant future. Medium-term investments include getting married, starting a business, paying for your children's education, or something similar. With medium-term investments, you have nothing to worry about the market volatility, which you can't afford in short-term investments.

You may also start introducing shares and bonds to your portfolio, as you'll have more time to grow your investments and longer to get over any downturns along the way.

Long-term goals

Long-term investments sit on the distant horizon, typically 9 to 10 years away or more. It's out of sight, but not out of mind. This occurred whenever you reinvest any returns, alongside your initial investment, to get further returns in the future. It also means you're ready to diversify your portfolio, including a mixture of assets that provide a healthy blend of risk and return, and with sensible protection and varied exposure.

Relatively speaking, time is on your side, so you ought to be ready to last out the volatility of the market.

Risk and return

When people mention risk, they're usually about market risk. Investing within the stock exchange is often volatile due to uncontrollable events like an economic downturn, political upheaval, or a natural disaster that will cause large price swings.

Market risk varies counting on what you invest in. Emerging markets are considered riskier than developed markets. so many other risks to think about, such as currency risk (fluctuating exchange rates) and longevity risk (the risk that will outlive your savings). No investment comes without risk, and there's always the prospect you'll revisit but you invest. As a rule of thumb, the more risk you're taking, the upper the potential return should be. While equities are seen because the highest-risk traditional investment, they need over the very future delivered the strongest returns. It's important to think twice about what proportion risk you're comfortable taking over. If, for example, you're on the brink of retirement, you'll want to avoid any big losses just before you're taking your money out.

Asset allocation simplifies how you split your money between different investment types like bonds, cash, shares, and property. There's an extensive choice of investments to settle on from, so you would like to know the risks related to each.

This will assist you to understand your approach to investment risk and determine the acceptable asset allocation for your investment goals.

CHAPTER TWO

Easy Areas you need to figure on before Escaping the Corporate World

One of the most major mistakes you can make is getting trapped within the moment, for example, running your idea or opportunity and spending time and money on developing it instead of taking a step back and thinking to yourself, "Is this the accurate time for me to be doing this?" or, "Am I ready for this challenge?"

Many people rush into a business venture, or peer pressure, or simply on a whim, and sometimes they have made a significant investment with their hard-earned capital only to understand they ought to have waited for a more opportune time, or done more research on homework on their state of affairs, before jumping straight into something they were ill-prepared for.

Being 'ready' means you recognize opportunities within your environment as an individual, your purpose in life, and what you will like to be in life.

The Secret and famous human potential movement teach us some areas of life that you simply want to master. These areas are:

1. Financial (money and wealth)

2. Physical (fitness and activity)

3. Mental (learning and personal development)

4. Social (environment) Physical (fitness and activity)

5. Vocational (career and business)

6. Family (relationships)

7. Spiritual (belief and mindfulness)

It's an honest exercise to review these 7 areas by yourself to ascertain if there's a fit with what you're trying to achieve and where you currently are. They're all inter-related and the maximum amount as you'll want to shift your focus in business success, it could come at the price of your finances, your health, and/or your relationships. It's worth having a mentor to chat with if you're seriously looking for a major shift in your life and moving ahead. You must be in a position of stability and mental strength before embarking on this journey. By being 'ready for the challenge, you bring your state thereto of a champion before a race – you've done your homework and all the preparation and now you're ready to run the marathon.

CHAPTER THREE

The Ultimate Truth Most People Ignore That Will Determine Your Level Of Success

Go hard or go home, there is no room for playing small. Settling for a life that is below what you are capable of living. You've chosen more workload of building a business, add to your current job - this is a great undertaking! It's going to stretch you in every human way possible, financially, time, physically with all the additional hours you'll get to put in, Ironically when times get tough and even spiritually, you will need inspiration elsewhere to maneuver that day when it seems hopeless.

So...the question is!

This has to be an excellent purpose that drives you every day to get out of bed and be motivated. When times get challenging and if you are strong enough, will be the sole thing that carries you forward at that moment.

You constantly got to challenge your WHY and see if it's as strong as you think that it's and if it is for the long term ...not just a feel-good wish of yours. Your WHY will fuel your passion and this may begin in every action you undertake. Follow your heart. Be a part of something positive. Do something that matters. this might be anything – big or small, local or global, personal or world-changing. The key thing is that its meaning for you. Don't ever accept or settle for less.

CHAPTER FOUR

The One Obsession All Successful People Share That Completely Destroys Procrastination

Ever wonder how some people seem to manage it all with ease and grace? they might be running several successful businesses, have a family with young kids, travel for work, and still seem to possess time for enjoying sports and social life. They somehow manage to suit it into their day, which incidentally contains an equivalent 24 hours we all have. So how do they are doing it?

Well, they're no different to you or me. they only prioritize their time differently and are hooked on going to where they're going and won't take no for a solution.

It's what you select to try to do together with your 24 hours throughout your time, that determines how or once you will get to realize your goals. the great news is that prioritization may be a discipline and thus a skill that will be learned. You face multiple choices a day, from what you wear, what you select to eat and drink, how you travel, who you accompany, how productive you're at work, what you are doing once you click, what books you read, what you hear, what you watch, what proportion time you spend on social media and what time you sleep. Your life is a huge web of choices and every single choice leads you on a particular path. Sometimes when things get busy, you'll end up taking over too many things and sometimes sacrificing important things like sleep within the process. In business, prioritizing is one of the essential skills that you simply will get to master to form the absolute best use of your efforts and the people of your team. It's also necessary as you are doing this, to permit yourself the power to make calmness and space in your life so that you'll focus your energy and a spotlight on the items that matter.

When you are focused on your business, things automatically become easier, you grind to a halt less often, you don't need to push as hard to start out making inroads.

Learning to mention 'no' to things may be a skill that will assist you to save valuable time and money at the end of the day. It'll also help bring you to your goals and dreams quicker because you'll be laser-focused on achieving outcomes. Taking continuous action can assist you to beat procrastination and move forward in your business. This needs discipline and like athletes training for the Olympic Games, it's just a matter of doing an equivalent thing over and once again, till you form a habit and practice eventually becomes perfect. Business never sits still in an ever-changing environment and neither must we. When unsure of what to try to do, return to your goals and do the priority actions which will take you one step closer to achieving those goals.

CHAPTER FIVE

The science of getting rich

WHATEVER could also be said in praise of poverty, the truth is that it's impossible to measure a complete or successful life unless one is comfortable. No man can rise to his greatest possible height in talent or soul development unless he has wealth; for to unfold the soul and to develop talent he must have many things to use, and he cannot have this stuff unless he has money to purchase them with.

Society is design to the extent that man must have money in other to become the possessor of things, i.e. a man must develop in mind, soul and body by utilizing different opportunities. The aim of all life is personal development, and any goal and objective attached to a man must be a science of getting rich.

The greater achievement in life is development; man must work hard in other to attain the predetermined development. The right to life means having the unrestricted use of all the necessary things, like mental, spiritual, and physical.

In this book, I will literary speak about riches figuratively, riches doesn't mean you are contented or satisfied with the little you have.

The person who guarantees all he needs for the living of all the life is rich, and no man who has not a ton of money can have all he needs. Life has progressed up until now, and become so mind-boggling, that even the first normal man or lady requires a lot of abundances to live in a way that even methodologies culmination. each one normally needs to turn out to be all that they are fit for turning into; this craving to comprehend inborn potential outcomes is intrinsic in human instinct; we won't assist energetic with being all that we can be. Achievement in life is becoming what you need to be; you can become what you might want to be exclusively by utilizing things, and you'll have the free utilization of things just as you become rich enough to search for them. To comprehend the study of getting rich is in this manner the most fundamental of all information.

Nothing wrong in wanting to get rich in fact getting rich is the goal. Craving for wealth is the desire for a richer and more bountiful life; and that desire is praise worthy.

We live based on these three motives; we live for the body, we live for the mind, we live for the soul. None of these is best or better than the other; all are working together, and none of the three-body, mind, or soul -- can function very well if either of the others is not functioning very well. It is not right or noble to measure just for the soul and deny the mind or body, and it's wrong to measure for the intellect and deny body or soul.

We are familiar with the odious outcomes of living for the body and denying both mind and soul; and we see that genuine method the total articulation of all that man can give forward through body, mind, and soul. Whatever he can say, no man can be truly glad or fulfilled except if his body is living completely in each capacity, and except if the equivalent is valid for his psyche and his spirit. Any place there is unexpressed chance, or capacity not performed, there is unsatisfied longing. Want is plausibility looking for articulation, or capacity looking for execution.

Man can't live completely in the body without great food, open to apparel, and warm shelter; and without independence from unnecessary work. Rest and diversion are likewise important to his physical life. He can't live completely as a top priority without books and time to examine them, without a promising circumstance for movement and perception, or without intellectual companionship.

To live completely as a top priority he should have intellectual entertainments and should encircle himself with every one of the objects of workmanship and magnificence he is equipped for utilizing and appreciating.

CHAPTER SIX

To live completely in the soul, man should have love; and love is denied articulation by destitution.

A man's most elevated bliss is found in the bestowal of advantages on those he cherishes; love tracks down its generally regular and unconstrained articulation in giving. The one who has nothing to give can't fill his place as a spouse or father, as a resident, or as a man. It is in the utilization of material things that a man discovers full life for his body, fosters his mind, and unfurls his spirit. It is in this way of incomparable significance to him that he ought to be rich.

It is completely correct that you want to be rich; in case you are a typical man or lady you can't resist the urge to do as such. It is correct that you should concentrate on the Study of Getting Rich, for it is the noblest and generally fundamental, all things considered. If you disregard this examination, you are neglected in your obligation to yourself, to God and mankind; for you can deliver to God and humankind no more assistance than to benefit as much as possible from yourself.

THERE is a Study of getting rich, and it is an accurate science, similar to variable-based math or number-crunching. There are sure laws that administer the way toward getting wealth; when these laws are learned and complied with by any man, he will get rich with numerical assurance.

The responsibility for property comes because of getting things done with a specific goal in mind; the individuals who get things done in this Specific Manner, regardless of whether deliberately or unintentionally, get rich; while the individuals who don't get things done in this Specific Manner, regardless of how hard they work or how capable they are, stay poor.

It is a characteristic law that causes consistently produce like outcomes; and, consequently, any human who figures out how to get things done in this specific manner will get rich.

The above assertion is valid and reality:

Getting rich doesn't involve climate, for, in case it was, every individual in specific areas would become well off; individuals of one city would all be rich, while those of different towns would all be poor; or the occupants of one state would move in abundance, while those of a bordering state would be in neediness.

In any case, wherever we see rich and helpless living next to each other, in a similar climate, and frequently occupied with similar employments. At the point when two men are in a similar area, and a similar business and one gets rich while the other remains are poor, it shows that getting rich isn't, basically, a question of climate. A few conditions might be better than others, yet when two men in a similar business are in a similar area, and one gets rich while the other fizzles, it demonstrates that getting rich is the aftereffect of getting things done with a particular goal in mind.

Furthermore, the capacity to get things done in this specific manner isn't expected exclusively to the ownership of ability, for some individuals who have incredible ability stay poor, while other people who have almost no ability get rich.

Considering rich people, they are average individuals in all aspects, they are not better than other men. it is very clear that they are rich not because of their abilities or talent but because they get things done in a unique and certain way.

Getting rich isn't the consequence of saving, or "thrift"; many exceptionally penurious individuals are poor, while free spenders regularly get rich.

Getting rich is not doing what other people refuse to do; for two men in a similar business regularly do the very same things, and one gets rich while the other remaining poor or bankrupt.

From these explanations, we can conclude that getting rich is the result of doing things in a Certain and unique Way.

If getting rich results from doing things in a Certain and unique Way, and if like causes always produce like effects, then any man or woman who can do things in their way can become rich. Therefore, the whole matter is brought within the domain of natural science.

The question arises here, whether this Certain Way may not be so complex that only a couple may follow it. Skillful people get rich, unskillful also get rich; intellectually brilliant people get rich, and foolish people get rich; physically strong people get rich, and weak and sickly people get rich.

These can be true, as we have seen, so far as natural ability is concerned.

The ability to think, reason, and understand is, of course, essential, but in so far as natural ability is concerned, any man or woman who has sense enough to read and comprehend these words can be rich.

Also, we have seen that it is not a matter of the environment. Location counts for something; one wouldn't attend the guts of the Sahara and expect to try to a successful business. If anybody in your area can get rich, so can you, and if anybody else in your area can get rich, so you too.

Again, it's not a matter of selecting some particular business or profession.

You will indeed do best during a business you wish, which is pleasant to you, and if you've got specific talents that are well developed; you will do best in a company that involves the exercise of these talents.

Be that as it may, besides these overall constraints, getting rich isn't subject to your participating in some specific business; however, upon your figuring out how to get things done with a particular goal in mind. If you are currently in business, and any other person in your territory is getting wealthy in a similar industry, while you are not getting rich, you're not getting things done inside the same Way that the contrary individual is doing them.

No one was prevented from getting rich by lack of capital. True, as you accumulate wealth, the increase becomes more accessible and rapid; but one who has wealth is already wealthy and does not need to think about how to become so. Regardless of how poor you'll be, if you start to try to dodo things within the Certain Way, you'll begin to urge rich; and you'll begin to possess capital. The getting of wealth may be a neighborhood of the method of getting rich, and it's a part of the result.

CHAPTER SEVEN

Perpetually follows the doing of things in the Specific Manner.

You might be the imperfect man on the landmass and be profoundly in the red; you might have neither one of the companions, impact nor assets, however if you start to get things done this way, you should dependably begin to get rich, for like causes should deliver like outcomes. If you have no capital, you'll get capital; in case you're inside some unacceptable business, you can get into the proper organization; in case you're in some unsuitable area, you can go to the right spot; and you'll do as such by starting in your current business and in your present location to get things done in the Specific Manner which causes achievement.

NO man is poor because opportunity has been removed from him; other people have monopolized the wealth and fence it. You may be shut off from engaging in business in certain lines, but other channels hospitable you. Probably it might be hard for you to urge control of any of the great railroad systems; that field is pretty much monopolized. But the electrical railway business remains in its infancy and offers many scopes for the enterprise. It'll be but a really few years until traffic and transportation through the air will become an excellent industry, and altogether its branches will give employment to many thousands, and maybe to millions, of people. Why not turn your attention to the development of aerial transportation instead of competing with Top individual et al. for an opportunity within the steam railway world?

It is a significant fact that in case you are a worker in the utilize of the steel trust, you have practically no shot at turning into the proprietor of the plant in which you work; yet it is likewise a fact that on the off chance that you initiate acting with a particular goal in mind, you can before extended leave the utilize of the steel trust; you can purchase a ranch of from ten to forty sections of land, and have a connection in business as a maker of staples. There is a massive chance as of now for men who will live upon tiny plots of land and develop the equivalent seriously; such men will get rich. You'll say that you can't get the ground; however, I will demonstrate to you that it isn't unthinkable and that you can positively get a homestead on the off chance that you go to add a specific Way.

At various periods, the tide of change sets in multiple ways, steady with the crucial necessities.

Accordingly, a specific phase of social development has been reached. In America, it is putting toward agribusiness and the united ventures and callings. Today, the chance is open before the assembly line laborer in his line. It is accessible before the money manager who supplies the rancher totally before the person who gives the assembly line laborer; and before the expert man who holds up upon the rancher more than before the person who serves the work.

Opportunity is bountiful for the individual who will go with the tide instead of attempting to swim against it. So the assembly line laborers, either as people or as a class, aren't denied the opportunity. The laborers are not being "held down" by their lords; they are not "ground" by the trusts and mixes of capital. As a class, they are there because they don't get things done with a particular goal in mind. On the off chance that the laborers of America decided to do as such, they could follow the occurrence of their siblings in Belgium and different nations and set up extraordinary retail chains and co-employable enterprises; they may choose men of their group for the workplace and pass laws preferring the advancement of such co-usable areas, and in a couple of years, they could take serene ownership of the industrial field.

The law of abundance is something similar to all things considered for all others. They should learn these; and that they will remain where they're the length of they do as they do. The individual specialist, be that as it may, isn't held somewhere near his group's obliviousness or psychological lethargy; he can follow the tide of freedom to wealth, and this book will disclose to him how. Nobody is kept in poverty by shortness within the supply of riches; there is more than enough for all.

It is even as easy to realize financial success, and to urge rich your own way, because it is to struggle and remain poor. By working a touch harder at the start, you'll enjoy vastly greater rewards afterward. Once you begin practicing a number of the ideas during this book, you'll launch yourself toward financial independence. You'll become one among most affluent people in your community. You'll have the house, the car, the life-style, the checking account, the inner satisfaction, the pride and therefore the self-esteem that accompany great success. It is all up to you. Good luck!

Conclusion

Breaking free from financial dispute isn't easy, and every folks has got to make the choice for ourselves.

Having come this far, you ought to feel more confident in your ability to maneuver during a new direction and leave the company scene once and for all. This may open up opportunities for you to make a life for yourself on your own terms, and take responsibility for your outcomes.

Starting a business is often one among the foremost challenging things you do due to the high level of uncertainty. its help business look great, as there are numerous opportunities out there waiting to be explored and other people that you simply can help and make a difference with.

Treating business during a professional manner will offer you a way higher likelihood of success. a bit like professional sport, or browsing parenting for the primary time, if you're ready to get the proper help and advice from coaches, mentors and other people who are there before, you'll save many headaches, time and valuable money and 'fast-track' where you would like to travel , instead of trying to work it all out on your own. this is often probably the most important mistake most new business owners fail to acknowledge early .

www.ingramcontent.com/pod-product-compliance
Lightning Source LLC
Chambersburg PA
CBHW070141230526
45472CB00004B/1631